NAGUAL

Raúl Nicolás Camacho

NAGUAL

It has been a month since I separated from one of the many families I have lived with over the two centuries I have been in this world. The taste of unsweetened coffee I drink every morning reminds me of the bitterness of my existence; I think of my past and only wish day after day to find the end and accept the price I must pay for once having wished to be what I am.

I have had to live these years in different ways, sometimes rich and powerful, other times as the poorest of men; sometimes lonely, sometimes with a large family, but always, sooner or later, I have to keep occupying the place I should have left for someone else.

The only way I can free myself from this curse is by finding a descendant of mine, and I am not even sure if one exists. The hope of finding them fades day by day, and the resignation to continue living this way pushes me to enjoy what I do when I have to keep taking the place of those who could have accepted mine.

Three weeks ago, I spoke with a priest to tell him the story of my life. The rain was falling, reminding me of who I am, while I paid attention to the people leaving the church, looking surprised that it was raining in the middle of summer and that darkness was present at such an early hour in the afternoon.

The religious images in the church looked empty, without that divine glow that sharpens the senses easily when one has firm faith. While the last people were leaving, I went into the confessional. The priest who would listen to my words was preparing to sermonize me, kissed his purple stole, and put it over his shoulders, leaving the gold-embroidered crosses on the front.

I knew he would not believe me when I told him what my life has been like. For many people, only God can punish us for our sins. He breathed deeply, letting me feel the fatigue he had from the long hours of work he had spent, and began.

—Hail Mary Most Pure.

—Conceived without sin —I replied, following the custom. With a relaxed voice and a calm, soft tone, as if to give me confidence to bare my soul, he continued.

—Tell me your sins, my son.

—Father, my soul is condemned to burn in hell, and I have not the slightest hope of salvation.

—My son, we all have salvation if we truly repent and seek God's forgiveness, He can save us! —he answered, trying to comfort my fears.

—No, Father! Not in my case, because I do not repent for what I have done, the only difference is that now I have to follow orders. I have become a slave and cannot defy my master! —I replied, recalling my past.

—What do you mean? What are you talking about? Who is your master? —the priest asked me, puzzled.

—For you to understand, Father, I need to tell you how it all began —I replied without stopping looking at him through the transparent black cloth of the wooden wall that separated us. He, accustomed to hearing stories from different people, spoke to me calmly and in a challenging tone.

—All right, my son, I am listening. —I sighed deeply.

—Father, it was December of 1809 when my life began to change.

—Wait! Wait! We are in 2013, are you telling me that you are over two hundred years old? That's impossible, no one can live that long! —he rebuked me, thinking I was joking.

—Then you do not accept what is written in the Bible about Moses or even Abraham, who lived many years, was that also impossible? —I challenged his beliefs.

—Well, my son, Abraham and Moses were chosen by God to fulfill divine commands, that's why God gave them the time necessary for their mission —he tried to tell me not to compare myself to them.

—And you do not believe that I am in a similar situation, but on the opposite side.

—All right, go on, I will not interrupt you anymore.

—I began to tell him the story of my life, and he prepared to listen to me with the certainty that I would only tell him lies.

NAGUAL

—Father, at that time I was already a married man, my wife was pregnant, and although we were very poor, happiness and love were part of our home. We eagerly awaited the birth of our child; I worked as a laborer on one of the richest estates to the south, now past the border, in a town in the Mezquital Valley, in the Intendancy of Mexico. The owner of that estate was a Spaniard, greedy and despotic, who only thought about how to get richer at our expense, his workers. We all had to call him Don Miguel. He was a hypocritical and cold man; the only person he possibly felt any affection for was his wife, Doña Lucía, who was also pregnant. It was only a matter of days before she too would give birth. What was happening in that place had ceased to matter to me; the only thing occupying my mind were thoughts of the family I had begun to form. Unlike me, everyone who worked and lived on the estate was very excited about the celebration that would take place at the end of the day. Doña Lucía was meticulously checking the details for the preparations of the birthday party that would be in honor of Don Miguel. Everything had to be ready by eight in the evening because that was when the guests would start to arrive. Most of them were Spaniards, the most important people, and the wealthy of that region were the ones chosen for the gathering. I was chopping wood for the fire, as I had to supply the cooks who were preparing the various dishes. Román, the foreman, approached me, looking at me with disdain.

—You can leave once you're done! Román walked away, slapping against his leg the whip he always carried in his hand to drive his horse or to punish us. He was a ruthless, inhuman man. All of us who worked under his orders were afraid of him; there was not one of us who dared contradict him. But despite his character and the disdain he showed for the indigenous people, I felt he was harsher with me than with the others when it was my turn to be punished. Without paying much attention to Román's offensive words, I hurried to finish my work, but when it was time to return home, a terrible anxiety began to invade me, I sensed that something bad was about to happen. I returned the ax I had been using to a little room we used as a storeroom. We all had to return the tools we had used during our shift, or else it would be deducted from our wages. I left quickly and didn't even say goodbye to my colleagues. I wanted to get home as soon as possible, but no matter how much I hurried, it would take me at least an hour and a half.

At that time, I had already built a small house ten months earlier. That was how long I had been living with Sara, my wife. Due to the poverty in which I had grown up, I had no other choice but to find a place far from the town where the land had no owner and build something to live in with my love. I never knew my parents and I don't know if I had siblings. The only thing I remember, since I can recall, is that I was working in that same place, Don Miguel's Hacienda. The payment I received when I was a child was only food, once or twice a day, and a place to sleep in the stable, next to the horses. I knew the inside of the estate perfectly, my age and the innocence of my actions allowed me to sneak around the corners. Sometimes they would catch me, and Román would punish me, but I didn't care because that was the only fun I had. My favorite place was the chapel of the estate, where I would hide to play, thinking I could talk to God, that I was one of His angels and that He sent me to punish the bad ones who made good people suffer. As I shortened the distance to my house, I was remembering how my childhood had been.

When I arrived, my wife was lying down and told me she wasn't feeling well; I thought it was just the usual discomforts that pregnant women have, but it still worried me. "Don't worry, it will pass," she reassured me. I lay down beside her, trying to comfort her, and began to tell her about my workday and how happy I was to be back with her. Not even an hour had passed since I arrived when the wind started to blow very hard, and the candles that were lighting us went out; the sky was thundering, discharging lightning that shook the ground and the noise reverberated in our ears. It started to rain very hard, water was coming in from all sides, because the house was made of simple logs and dry branches, and the roof was made of palm leaves. I thought everything would collapse, and before I knew it, water was already starting to run on the floor; the dirt floor had turned into a small stream. I prepared to go out and cover the path of the water that was crossing our home, but it stopped raining. "It's over, tomorrow I'll find a safer place." "Everything is starting to get complicated," my wife said, putting her hands on her belly. "Our child is about to be born." I couldn't believe that, at this difficult moment, my child wanted to come into this world. "Are you sure?" I asked my wife, wanting to hear the opposite.

"Yes! The pains have started, please go get the midwife, we still have time." I kissed her on the forehead. "I'll be back soon, I promise." I ran out; as I moved away, I heard her screams, tearing my soul apart. "Please, my God, help me! Take care of her and let me get help."

I stumbled and slipped, my bare feet getting destroyed in the desperate race I was running; my body got injured as I fell on the stones of the path. The branches of thorny bushes tangled around me, tearing my skin and clothes. The blood dripping from my head blinded me, and I fell again. All I could think about was saving my wife and my child. I knocked on the midwife's house with all my strength, screaming and kicking the door, desperate because I wouldn't arrive in time to help my wife. Endless minutes passed until I realized that no one was there. I remembered it was Don Miguel's party, and one of the guests was a doctor—he was my only hope. It was half an hour away, and perhaps on the way back, Don Miguel would help by lending me horses, making it quicker to get aid for my wife. "Thank you, my God, this is for the best. If I didn't find the midwife, it's because You willed it this way, because now I'll get a doctor, and I can return sooner," I thought as I ran. The carriages of the guests were everywhere; the coachmen had gathered around fires to keep warm while waiting for the party to end so they could transport their masters. At the main entrance, Román grabbed me by the arm.

"Where do you think you're going? You can't go in and you won't bother anyone inside. Only important and decent people can pass, and you're a filthy Indian. Get lost, you wretch." With a push, he sent me sprawling to the ground. Without time to get up, he smashed his foot into my face, and I felt like I was losing consciousness. As best as I could, I got on my knees and tried to explain that I needed help, but all I received in response were more blows. His whip left me with wounds that mixed with those I had already inflicted on myself in my desperation to get help. Finally, Román grabbed me by the hair and dragged me to the middle of the pathway, delivering another blow to my face. "You'll be lucky if the boss doesn't fire you tomorrow when I tell him you tried to enter his house without permission." The onlookers didn't give much importance to a laborer being beaten. "Why, my God? Don't leave me alone, please," I muttered. It occurred to me to enter the house from another side; I knew it perfectly, it wouldn't be difficult. All I had to do was get to the doctor, and he would help me. I jumped over the back of the house to one of the balconies, opened the window, and I was inside. I slid towards the main hall, running out of strength, supporting myself on the walls to keep moving. My blood was staining them. As I descended the stairs, no one noticed my presence until I reached the room where everyone was gathered. I tried to speak, but a lady, seeing my terrible appearance, screamed in fright. The commotion was so great that everyone in the room fell silent and stared at me. I approached the doctor as best as I could. As I knelt before him, explaining my situation and begging him to help me, my master Don Miguel was shouting for Román; the foreman quickly reached where I was and tried to hit me, but the doctor, with a hand signal, stopped him. "How do you plan to pay me? I don't think you have enough money! I don't accept chickens or eggs." The guests began to laugh. The humiliation I felt was immense, but not as much as the worry of knowing my last hope was gone. "Now I just have to get back to my wife," I thought. A lot of time had passed, and I didn't know how she was doing. With me kneeling, the foreman began to beat me. "I'll show you how to teach an Indian to respect the privacy of a home! Bring him, Román! Drag him to the yard!" Don Miguel would use me as an example. The foreman drove me out with lashes as if I were an animal; the water fountain in the center of the yard would be the site. As they finished tying me up, the foreman ordered one of his aides to bring a bucket of water and coarse salt. I couldn't imagine what awaited me; I was only thinking of my loved ones.

As I pleaded for forgiveness, the foreman dipped a rope into the bucket. All the guests were already gathered around, waiting for the punishment to begin. Román approached, tearing off what remained of my cotton shirt. What more damage could they do to me when my body had wounds everywhere? The only thing keeping me going was the concern for my wife. Román lashed the rope against my bare back; the salt made me writhe in pain. He became more and more vicious. He seemed to enjoy every blow he dealt while the guests laughed non-stop, enjoying the spectacle as if they were witnessing the punishment of the worst beast. Gradually, everyone observing the brutal act left, until only my executioner and

I remained. During the flogging, Román only struck my back. He handled the rope with great skill, like a whip, and in the last blow he delivered, he aimed the rope at my head, and it wrapped around my neck, unleashing more force at the end, bursting my lips. I lost consciousness. The next day, my body was completely numb; the cold night and the icy water from the fountain had acted as a kind of anesthesia; I felt no pain, but I couldn't move either.

With great effort, I slowly turned my head from side to side, trying to find someone who would take pity on me. I could barely see; my eyelids were swollen from the blows, and the water in the fountain was entirely red from the blood from my wounds. When I thought I might spend the day tied to that fountain, a worker who was about to start his shift approached me; I didn't even recognize him, I just thanked him when he cut my bonds with his machete. "We know what happened to you. Please, go and never come back." He helped me to my feet, and as best as I could, I moved away, wanting to reach my home. My body was becoming less numb; the stinging from the blows increased, making the journey more painful and seemingly endless. The anguish of not knowing if my wife was okay grew each time I fell to the ground. I begged God to help me get there and that she was alright.

NAGUAL

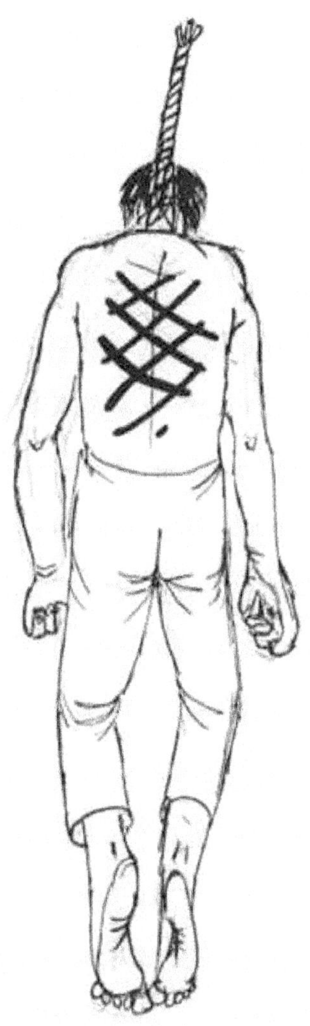

I will never forget the sight when I opened the door to my house. The blood my wife lost giving birth had attracted a pack of hungry coyotes. My son and she were torn apart, scattered everywhere. The coyotes had made holes in the ground, weakened by the previous night's rain. The darkest moment of my life was before me. I fell to my knees and began to cry, looking around, searching for an explanation for such cruelty.

"Why, why?" I collapsed, writhing in the suffering of my soul. The blood from my wounds began to flow again, mixing with theirs, spilled on the ground. I wanted to die.

I stood up with tears in my eyes and looked at the wooden cross hanging on the wall; I grabbed it forcefully, slamming it and stomping on it repeatedly. I insulted it and spat on it, trying to rid myself of the faith I had held all my life. I cursed it and blamed it for my fate and that of my family.

I don't know how long I spent sobbing and cursing God while holding what was left of my loved ones in my arms. I walked back and forth, not knowing what to do. After several hours, I went to the back of the house, dug into the ground with my bare hands until my fingernails tore off, opening what would be their grave.

I returned inside the house, wrapped their remains in the blankets we used as covers, and carried them to the pit I had made. As I covered them with dirt, I couldn't stop asking for their forgiveness for leaving them alone, but to me, there was only one culprit: God.

The next evening, I had already decided I didn't want to continue living this miserable life; the hope I had for a happy life died with my family.

I tied a rope to the branch of a tree, stood on a chair, and tied the noose around my neck. Without thinking, I jumped, swinging in all directions. Lacking air, I began to lose consciousness, the moonlight fading into total darkness. In a final effort, I stretched out my arms to surrender to death.

I thought I was dead. I couldn't distinguish what or who that person was who accompanied me. They made me feel like we were flying. Unconscious, I had nightmares; I saw my loved ones torn apart; I woke up screaming, and in the few moments of lucidity, I perceived a man by my side healing my wounds, giving me a thick, bitter liquid to drink, speaking to me calmly.

"You're going to recover, boy; you're out of danger now."

I don't know how many days I spent in bed; when I started to walk, it felt strange, I didn't feel weak or tired, it seemed as if I had simply slept for a night, and everything had been a nightmare. I searched through the halls, trying to find the person I had seen. It was a very large house; I reached the dining room; behind a huge table, at the head, was that figure. He had food served for two, waiting for someone. Standing, he looked at me intently.

"I was expecting you, come, join me for a meal."

I was very surprised, how could he know I would arrive? I clearly distinguished the figure of the one who had been healing me.

He was very tall, his long black hair reaching below his shoulders. It seemed he could see to the depths of my soul; his eyes penetrated; they were so dark that, no matter how hard I tried, I couldn't distinguish his pupils. The skin on his face and hands was very white, with veins easily visible. He had an elegant, distinguished demeanor; his voice was strong, he spoke with firmness, commanding respect and confidence at the same time.

I began to ask without stopping to observe him.

"I brought you because I need you." I was confused.

"What could you want from me? I have nothing. Why didn't you let me die? That's the only thing I want, I have no one, I lost my world. I'm not interested in living anymore!"

"Let me tell you what I offer you. This house can be yours with everything I have," he replied firmly. I was overwhelmed by despair.

"What good is it if I can't get back the only thing I loved? You can't remove the bitterness I carry in my heart!"

"But I can give you something very special that will help ease it. You can avenge those who caused you what you feel. Make them pay double. They will never hurt you again; you will get whatever you want if you accept."

"How can that be possible?" I didn't believe it.

"Look at your hands, look at your body." Surprise overcame me. The marks of my wounds had disappeared, I didn't have a scratch or a single scar. "That's just the beginning; with each passing day, you will be stronger. You will have so much power that nothing and no one can stop you. You will do things that only in your dreams were possible." He took my arm to propel me outside. "Let's go for a walk."

Before I could ask where we were going, we were on some kind of main road; the way we came formed a cross with it. The full moon clearly illuminated, and the trees cast shadows that looked like sinister figures.

The noise of an animal's hooves broke the silence; the wind blew, and when it hit the tree branches, intense moans could be heard.

"Fear nothing of what you see. I will show you what I've been talking about, what I can offer you if you accept."

I looked towards where the noise was coming from. Someone was pulling a mule that refused to move; it snorted and neighed, afraid to take another step.

My companion began to recite something I didn't understand. He crouched on his heels and began to transform into a monstrosity. His bones cracked as if breaking, his roars chilled my blood, my heart raced, shivers ran through me over and over. I couldn't believe it. I wanted to run away, but despite the fear, something made me feel protected; I tried to trust that he wouldn't harm me. His body was that of a dog, of enormous size; he stood on his hind legs, and his eyes glowed like burning coals.

The mule driver didn't move, terrified by the howls. The shadow that covered us prevented him from seeing us. But the moon's reflection illuminated him perfectly. The aberration, with a great leap, stood in front of the poor wretch. The mule fled in terror, leaving its master alone, who prayed while backing away without taking his eyes off the anomaly. It followed him slowly, waiting for the moment to attack, knocking him down when he tried to turn and run. He screamed as he was torn from skin to bone.

I watched the merciless attack; the idea of gaining that power seduced me; I felt the desire for revenge. The good feelings I had began to disappear, and the darkness of evil covered my spirit.

I was fascinated by that diabolical scene; the ease with which the beast destroyed drew me into hatred towards those who caused my misfortune. It seemed the massacre had ended; he called me to approach, and I obeyed. The victim was still breathing. He looked at me intently.

"Isn't this what you want for those you hate? Do you want me to end this one's life? Do you dare to take my place and put the people you hate in this man's place? Answer!" The unfortunate man bled on the ground, looking at me pleading for mercy. I looked back at the beast, feeling no compassion for that wretch whose life was slipping away.

"I accept! I don't care about the price." The creature, with one bite, tore off his neck, separating the head, and slowly moved away from the body. We left the corpse and walked towards the house. The howls of coyotes could be heard, signaling to finish devouring what was left of that man.

We walked in silence. Before arriving, he transformed back into a human. I was amazed, but not afraid. We sat at the table where we had started talking.

"Tomorrow we will begin your initiation," he sounded satisfied. Without saying anything else, he left.

While we were having breakfast, I asked him if there was anyone else, who prepared the food, or who took care of the chores to keep the house in order.

"I only have the necessary servants. I don't like them being close to me, and each of them knows what they have to do. Don't be surprised if you only see me, and if you're wondering if I have family, the answer is no."

As I brought bites to my mouth, I was intrigued by how he read my thoughts.

"If you want to know something, ask directly," he said as soon as I finished thinking it. I tried to lower my gaze, embarrassed, but he wouldn't let me.

"Look, boy, you have to learn to show courage. You have no reason to feel inferior to anyone. Your strength and bravery lie in your pain; let it out. You will become a completely different person."

Each word he spoke gave me strength. Sometimes I wanted to drown in my sorrow, but he wouldn't let me; he transformed it into a desire for reparation until he made me forget the idea of wanting to kill myself.

He taught me to recite invocations that helped me control natural forces, like the rain and the wind, to move the clouds and cover the sun. When I could handle it perfectly, we started with the rites to achieve metamorphosis. We could resemble any animal we wanted. Our eyes would turn a very bright red, and our bodies would become larger than those of natural animals.

All the time, he corrected my way of speaking, my behavior, and explained the lifestyle of rich people to me. My outcast condition was becoming a thing of the past while my thirst for reparation grew.

"Get ready, we're going out. They're hosting a party at the estate of someone I want you to meet. I'll introduce you as my nephew. This will help you connect with people of supposed power and easily get to your enemies. Also, I want to give you a lesson that will be useful for your plans," he told me after months of teaching.

"Master, how should I address you? All this time, you haven't told me your name, nor I mine."

"I know your name; I don't need to ask. At the party, I'll give you a different name, and mine is Josaphat. The last days we will spend together are approaching. You are preparing to take the place I no longer need. From today, you and I will share what we think and say to other people or do with them; we will be able to know it without being in the same place. You will see what I see, and I will see what you see. We will even feel the same emotions. We won't need to ask each other any more questions; you'll know everything about me. Of the people you have marked, you cannot let any of their direct descendants live; they all must die by your hand of wrath. If the first person you marked dies for different reasons and leaves a child alive, you will be vulnerable. Only one of them can kill you, whether it's the first child of the one who died or anyone descending from him. And only as long as their soul remains pure will you be unable to touch them; they must first fall into mortal sin so you can kill them, ensuring they have no successors. You can choose who will be the last person from the families you want to end. And before you finish them off, you must find another person to whom you will teach what you have learned from me. Only you can decide when you want to die. While you take the time to decide, nothing and no one can eliminate you. But remember, you cannot let your enemy live, nor their children, nor their children's children if they have any."

When Master Josaphat told me all this, I thought everything was in my favor because I had already decided to make Don Miguel suffer the same way I had suffered.

"I understand, but how can I find another person who wants to take my place?"

"I found you, and it wasn't that hard. You will stumble upon someone who needs revenge. They just have to be a soul free of sin."

"But Master, how can I know if the person I choose will be pure?"

"You will feel it. A soul is free of sin as long as it doesn't know the difference between good and evil in its heart. Anyone who knows the difference before committing a reprehensible act will be aware that it is a sin and will know their soul must pay the consequences," he replied, placing his hand on my shoulder.

Without asking anything else, I went to my room to get ready. As always, the hot bath was ready, and the clothes I would wear were laid out on the bed. I approached the bathtub and put red rose petals in it; I did this every night as a ritual. The petals represented the bodies of my partner and my child, the red color symbolizing their blood that mixed with mine the day I lost them. I undressed in front of the mirror to look at my body, and vanity surrounded me like the greatest of slips, like the one that condemned Satan. I could hardly believe I was the same person who had grown up on Don Miguel's estate. There was no trace left of that humble native who only lived to serve others.

I submerged myself in the tub's water, wanting to drown my memories. After a few seconds underwater, I slowly began to lift my head. Relaxed, I started to have images in my mind, as if I were in another place but still aware of everything around me. The mental connection with Master Josaphat had begun. I was in him, seeing the inside of his rooms, lying on his bed after taking a bath. His door opened, and two beautiful women, dressed in transparent robes, approached him. The perfection of their faces and bodies exuded an infernal sensuality, irresistible, inviting to carnal perversion in all its extremes. They let their garments fall to the floor, revealing their nakedness. They awakened in me the desire to possess them; the sensation was real. I imagined those women with me and no one else.

One kissed me slowly, biting my lips gently while her hands ran through my hair, causing spasms of pleasure. Meanwhile, the other caressed my chest and legs; they moved with the precision of someone who knew every sensitive spot on my body, producing an indescribable delight. The woman who was kissing me sat on top of me, placing her legs on either side of me. The heat of her body ignited in me a lust like never before, and I let myself be swept into that whirlwind, plunging into total perversion. My essence was corrupting.

After satisfying my instincts, I got out of the tub, trembling and savoring the experience. I began to open my eyes as if I wanted to continue with those women, but upon seeing the water, that thought vanished. It was entirely red, looking like blood. When I dried off, I checked the towel for any signs that my body had lost vital fluid. I found nothing. Without further thought, I proceeded to dress. The clothes I would wear that night were the most elegant I had ever worn, but I didn't feel uncomfortable, as if that attire was mine and I had worn it before.

The Master and I left our rooms at the same time, facing each other. We observed each other, feeling as if he were my mirror, reflecting myself in his person. A carriage awaited us at the main door. We boarded and headed to our appointment.

When we arrived at the party, I felt the presence of someone I hated—it was the doctor who had refused to help me. The desire for revenge started coursing through my veins, but my master grabbed my arm. "Calm down, you'll have time for that. For now, just focus on studying the paths that will lead you to your retribution." It was hard to contain the impulse.

When we reached the main hall, people looked at us, murmuring softly; every word of respect and admiration was clearly heard. The master interrupted the murmuring. "Good evening, dear friends. I've known you for a long time; we've shared many pleasant moments together, like the only family that has accompanied me during the solitude in which I have lived. Now, I have the pleasure of introducing you to my nephew, Antonio Vizcarra, who has come from Spain and is determined to stay and live with me. It will be an honor for you to accept him as you have accepted me. He and I are the same person, the same heart, and the same feelings. I also want to thank my friend Sebastián Bocanegra, the owner of this house, who allowed me to make this introduction to you. This gathering, as you already know, was made especially for you to meet my nephew." They began to applaud, and some approached, greeting me and welcoming me.

"It will be an honor for us to offer your nephew our friendship, in the same way we have offered it to you and you have accepted it," they said one after another.

Finally, the hosts of the house approached; Bocanegra was the last person I wanted to talk to. After showing off his wife, he put his arm around my shoulder and invited me to tour the hall, introducing me personally to his most important guests. Don Miguel was not there that night. He asked me a few questions as we stepped aside. He took two glasses of wine and offered me one, wishing to speak privately.

"What do you do? How do you make a living?"

"I'm a veterinarian," I sighed deeply to calm my hatred. He began to laugh.

"How do you plan to make money treating animals? They can't pay you. I have many heads of cattle and some horses; if one gets sick, I either sacrifice it or let it die and give the meat to those Indians in exchange for work. That way, I don't have to pay anyone and still come out ahead." He clearly showed the kind of scoundrel he was; nothing and no one mattered to him more than his money, which made my blood boil. "Let me tell you something. Once, I was enjoying a gathering at a friend's house when suddenly, a filthy Indian was begging me to help him because his wife was about to give birth. That poor wretch had nothing, not even the means to fall dead, do you think it was worth it to leave to help that wretch? These Indians are beasts." He spoke arrogantly and pompously.

I clenched my fists, trying not to kill him right there. I smiled slightly as I began to study him. "Do you have children, Doctor?" He took a long sip of wine from his glass, not wanting to answer.

"Antonio," he looked me in the eyes, "one must face the consequences of a poor choice. The woman I married is not fit to have children. I know they laugh behind my back, blaming me, saying I am not a real man. It is a shame I have had to live with. I tell you this because I feel the same trust with you as with your uncle. I don't know why, but Josaphat is right when he says you and he are the same person."

"I believe so," I replied. I knew the topic made him uncomfortable and that there was something more shameful, a problem no man would admit. I decided to have some fun. "You're a doctor; is there nothing you can do for your wife to help her conceive?"

"No, Antonio," his face was red, "I've tried everything, but it's been useless. There are things medicine can't cure. I've resigned myself to living like this. Now, I only care about money, and even if I don't have an heir, it doesn't bother me anymore. Let's end this conversation. Enjoy the party, talk with the others. And let me recommend, tonight many friends have brought their daughters who are of age to find a husband. Take advantage, you might find love in this place, but be careful not to end up like me."

"Don't worry, tonight I will dedicate myself to studying how to corner my prey."

"Well said, boy!" He took my comment as a joke. "Make yourself at home. If you need anything, take it. Allow me to attend to the other guests."

"Go ahead, I assure you I will indeed take what I desire," I responded, following his tone.

With the other guests, we discussed various topics. My master had told them I was the son of a sister of his who lived in Spain. I knew this; our mental connection was getting stronger, and we agreed on what we were asked.

After a long while, the master bid farewell to everyone, claiming he felt very exhausted, but that I would stay with them and he would send for me later. "I hope this night is unforgettable, thank you." I knew what he meant; he left, and we continued to share cheerfully. Fascinated by my presence, especially the women, the men who had brought their daughters spoke highly of them, how wonderful they were and how good they would be as wives. They invited me to visit them whenever I wanted. They knew my supposed uncle had no other family and that I would likely inherit his great fortune. Some, while saying goodbye, asked not to be forgotten.

The wealthy families were Spanish, and it was very difficult for young women to find a good match. Most of the time, they had to send their daughters to Spain to find a husband or bring one over. Many times, these were nobodies with invented titles, and only the family knew the truth. They tried at all costs not to mix with poor people to avoid comments and ridicule from society.

A servant approached to inform me that my carriage was ready whenever I needed it. I thanked him, and my host slapped him across the face. "How dare you insult my guest of honor! You're implying that he can leave now!"

"Sorry, that wasn't my intention." Embarrassed, he withdrew without turning his back on us, his eyes downcast. I felt the slap as if I had received it myself.

"You see the imprudence of these ignorant people; I tell you, they're like animals. Please accept my apologies."

"Don't worry, it doesn't matter to me; let's forget the incident."

We hadn't finished when we heard loud howls, as if an animal was in the stables, and the dogs were barking and howling. A terrified peon ran in, trembling, too agitated to speak clearly.

"Patron, close all the doors and windows of this house, a nagual is outside, it just killed several cows in the stable and might come this way."

"What are you saying, fool?" exclaimed the doctor. "Those howls can only be coyotes. Gather the peons and go chase those animals away."

"No, Patron, you don't understand," the peon argued, very scared, "no one will go out. We know they're not coyotes; it's a nagual. I saw it myself. You must have done something to bring it here."

"If you don't obey, you'll lose your jobs," he ordered, trying to hide his fear, while the last guests at the party crossed themselves.

"Better to lose our jobs than to face a nagual. Anyway, this house is already marked."

"Uneducated nonsense, like all your kind."

"If you don't believe me, Patron, go yourself, ask your guests to accompany you, so you can see for yourself what's out there."

"Shut up, you're making these fine people nervous."

"Patron, I've done my duty by warning you. May God have mercy on you, but don't ask me to go out until the dogs stop barking; only then can I know the nagual is gone."

The guests looked at each other, wanting to hear a reasonable answer to what they had heard from the peon who refused to set foot outside the house. The drivers had come into the house, and with the pages who were with us, they were praying in our native language, further disturbing the atmosphere.

"This night we will part ways. I must pay the price for what I am, and you will begin your tasks. You are ready; you have learned perfectly and will receive my power." He looked thoughtful but with an enormous calm, as if he were being freed from a heavy burden.

The hours passed very quickly. After sunset, he had already prepared the last ritual we would share. Before midnight, we went out; outside the house, he had built a bonfire in the center of the yard. In front of the fire, he recited a new spell, engraved in my being as if with a red-hot iron. He fell to his knees and extended his arms to form a cross. Through our mental connection, I felt as if I were in his place, including the blow to the knees as he let himself fall to the ground, which was only a slight hint of the real price I would pay to take his place.

The bonfire grew, producing shadows from which aberrations emerged, similar to the transformation he had undergone the night he offered me his power. They approached until they completely surrounded him, then leaped over him, clawing at him bit by bit until they brought him down. In unison, the beasts pounced on him, tearing him apart with their bites.

I felt his despair within me with every part torn off and devoured, experiencing the physical and emotional agony of my master firsthand. His memories flooded my mind, from his bitterness to his encounter with the demon that transformed him. I writhed on the ground with the pain that dragged him toward death. The images of how he found me revealed many things I didn't know. He had used his powers to cause the rain, the birth, and had attracted the pack of hungry coyotes to finish off my wife and child. He had been at the party, watched everything, and had been monitoring me until the moment I decided to take my life by hanging myself from that tree. The last images were of the previous night when I finished bathing, and the water had turned to blood. The spirits of my wife and child separated from me because they didn't want to follow the path I had chosen. The only person I had known since then, who I thought really wanted to help me, had deceived me.

When I finished feeling the beasts' attack, I tried to join them in the assault, but one of them stood before me, offering me the heart of my master. I took it with the same hatred I felt toward the doctor, Don Miguel, and Roman, and devoured it. I swallowed the muscle, feeling as if I were chewing my own flesh. When I swallowed the last piece of my master's heart, a strong heat emanated from the center of my guts, coursing through my body from head to toe as if it were the flames of hell. I collapsed on the ground, screaming, which turned into howls; uncontrollably, I transformed into the monster my master had been.

Our covenant was sealed. The spawns disappeared in the same way they had arrived, into the shadows. Completely alone, I prepared to use the absolute power I had gained.

I headed to Don Miguel's estate, to the cattle corrals. Roman liked to hunt and sleep in the open field, sleeping next to the campfires with a shotgun in hand to guard the cattle.

He was a mestizo. The Spaniards despised him for being the son of an indigenous woman, and Roman despised the indigenous people because he felt Spanish. To the rich men, mestizos were the best foremen; they treated the natives harshly and were as loyal as dogs to their masters.

Before approaching, I started howling; the cows got up and began walking around, looking for protection. Roman stood up, holding the shotgun, ready to shoot at anything. I ran howling, protected by the darkness, while he aimed his weapon at where he thought the animal scaring the cattle and himself was. I slowly emerged from the darkness to let myself be seen; when he had me in his sights, he fired without harming me. I pounced, running on all fours, leaping to land on him; he tried to flee but tripped, paralyzed by fear, unable to believe what he was seeing. With my front paws on his chest to immobilize him, I slowly brought my fangs to his face. The drool dripping from my snout fell on his face, terrifying him even more. Roman closed his eyes, resigned. I moved away and attacked the cows.

A swipe was enough for me; in seconds, I killed almost half. Finally, I caught a cow trying to flee, burying my fangs in its neck and, twisting my head, threw it through the air to land near Roman, who was paralyzed. As the animal bled out with its neck torn open, I walked away, satisfied with my display of strength.

Roman had no direct descendants; it would be easier to finish him off in the end. Although the doctor also had no children, I decided to leave Roman alive for a while so he could tell the others and fill them with terror, to live his last days afraid, thinking any night I would return for him.

On my way back to my nest, I passed through the village houses, climbing the rooftops, howling and making noise, scratching the walls, enjoying how people started praying while the dogs growled and tried to corner themselves at the doors, as if asking to be let in. I left my marks for easy notice. When I was far enough from the populated area, without stopping, I transformed into a crow to leave no trace.

At first light, one of the servants knocked on my chamber door, already prepared to attend to me with the same diligence and loyalty as they had done with Josafat. He informed me that Sebastián Bocanegra wanted to see me and was waiting in the reception room. I covered myself with a robe and went to find out.

"Sorry to bother you," he said after we greeted each other, noticeably nervous. "I asked for your uncle, but your servant told me that Josafat had to leave urgently for Spain. Really, it is you I want to talk to, Antonio."

"Well, doctor, please have a seat and tell me how I can help you," I said, showing a bit of concern.

"Antonio, do you remember what happened at my house before you left the party?" he sighed, worried.

"Yes, of course, Doctor Bocanegra."

"As soon as the sun came up, I gathered the people to find out what had happened in the stable. More than thirty of my cows were dead, dismembered, and the tracks we found from the animal that attacked them were very strange. I had never seen anything like it. The worst part is that all my workers left; they didn't want to help even to lift the bodies. I went out to get help, but no one wants to set foot on the estate. I even offered to give away the meat just to get them to take it, but no one wanted to go pick it up. Those ignorant people keep saying it was a nagual that killed my animals. I have come to ask for your help. You are a veterinarian; perhaps you can figure out what killed my livestock and tell those backward people to come back. I ask you, I beg you, come to my house. I will pay you very well, I promise you. If I don't do something soon, everything will collapse, and I will lose what I have achieved. Like you, I came from Spain, leaving everything to make a fortune, and I can't lose it now."

Seeing the man begging for help, as I once had, gave me satisfaction. His suffering was beginning.

"Count on me; I will come to your house as soon as I can," I made him feel that I was interested.

"Thank you, Antonio, I will be eternally grateful to you. I will leave now. Consider my house as your own."

I accompanied him to the exit to see him mount the horse he had arrived on. Even with all his money, he couldn't find anyone to drive his carriage.

45

On the way, I encountered many people heading to the church, terrified. They all spoke of the nagual's tracks; the town already knew about Bocanegra's house and Don Miguel's, which had also been abandoned. Before arriving, I recited to summon strong winds and erase the tracks left by the one who had been my master at Sebastián Bocanegra's estate, as well as the ones I had made the previous night at Don Miguel's.

The doctor was waiting for me outside, eager to show me the traces he had been talking about. In the stables, I examined the corpses while he paced back and forth, looking at the ground.

"It can't be, how could they disappear?"

"What are you talking about?" I asked him.

"The tracks, Antonio, I swear they were here, I saw them myself."

"Doctor, don't worry about the tracks if they're gone now," I said to confuse him further. "From what I've seen here, I can't tell what attacked them. A single animal, no matter how large, couldn't kill an entire herd. If there had been several, at least one would have been completely devoured, but coyotes don't attack such large animals."

"Please, Antonio, don't tell me you're going to believe what those Indians are saying too!" he protested, frustrated.

"Doctor, all I can say is that I don't see any other animal tracks to know more accurately what kind of creature killed your cattle. What I do recommend is that you get rid of the bodies; they've started to rot and could make the rest sick." Bocanegra continued pacing, desperate.

"But how? Not even you and I together can move them, and even if we cut them up one by one, it would take us a lot of time."

"Doctor, why don't you try getting some of your friends' workers?"

"Haven't you understood? None of those bastards want to come!"

"You just need one who knows how to harness a pair of oxen to drag them. Tie them together, set them on fire with wood, and that will solve this problem for now."

The doctor was completely convinced that no one would help him. With my words, I led him to think of Román; the doctor still didn't know that the same thing had happened there.

For the doctor to get from his place to Don Miguel's, he had to cross the town from one end to the other and then continue on horseback for two hours. Mine was halfway between the two, on the outskirts of the town. I didn't have to pass through the town to reach either of them. They raised cattle, sheep, and harvested fruits, and the doctor also practiced his profession occasionally with those who could pay for his services in the town or other estates. Unlike the two of them, Josafat only planted corn and beans seasonally and only hired laborers when necessary, so the only ones I had were personal servants. That's why the doctor didn't ask me to provide any of them.

"Román, he can help me," he said enthusiastically, as if the foreman would save his life. "That idiot thinks he's like us. Just to prove he's not like the Indians, he won't refuse to come. I'll go see Don Miguel and ask him to lend Román to me. By the way, you haven't met him yet; why don't you come with me? I'll introduce you."

"You go ahead, doctor. I could try to talk to the townspeople to convince them it was coyotes that caused this and get them to return. Another time, you can introduce me to your friend, if that's okay with you." I couldn't risk seeing him.

"Excellent idea, Antonio. It couldn't be better. Thank you, I hope to repay this debt very soon."

I had already decided to start collecting those debts that very night. Bocanegra wasn't sure of achieving what he had planned. The doctor's arrogance and haughtiness were fading, along with what remained of his life.

NAGUAL

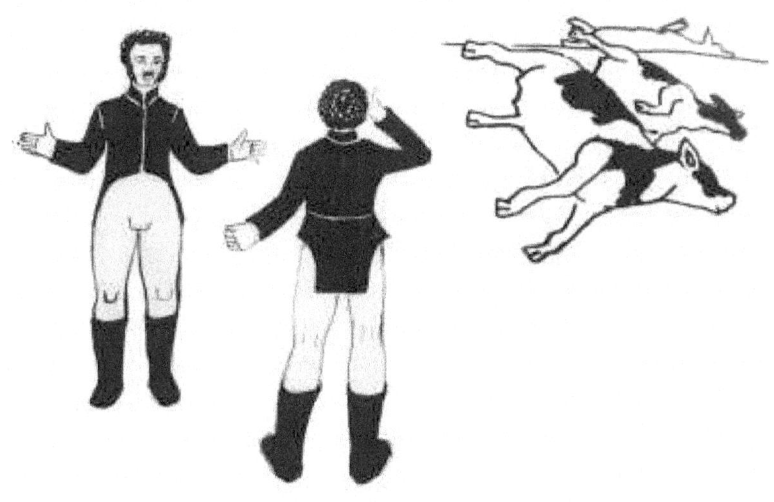

When he disappeared into the streets of the town, I headed for the church. There wasn't a soul on the street; everyone wanted to speak with the priest. I asked my driver to stop the carriage in front of it. I didn't get out; I just wanted to listen to what the people were saying to the Father. From outside, I could clearly hear what was being said; my senses were heightened by the power I had received.

It was enough for me to be in a place or with someone to know what was happening there or to that person without me being physically present. But I had to be in my human form at least once, which is why I wasn't worried about accompanying the doctor to know what would happen.

My delight in sowing fear was growing. Women were crying, and men were begging the priest to do something to expel the nagual from those places. They knew it was only looking for certain people, but if they encountered it, it might kill them too.

"Please, my children, calm down. What you heard last night might have been hungry coyotes."

"No, Father. The coyotes don't come close because they're afraid of the dogs, and it was the dogs that were scared last night. Besides, many of us saw the nagual's tracks. You have to do something."

"Please, there is no nagual; it's just your imagination, stories your parents or grandparents told you. Tell me, who has ever seen the nagual?"

"I have, Father. I was at Don Sebastián's estate two nights ago. He threw a party to welcome a nephew of Don Josafat. I went to the stable to check, and when I was about to go back to the house, I saw it jump over the corral and start killing the cows. I ran to tell the doctor, who didn't believe me, but just hearing the nagual's howls made him so scared he wouldn't move from where he was standing. He started scolding me and telling me to shut up, but I swear, Father, here before God, I'm not lying about what my eyes saw."

"Yes, it's true," said another, who worked at Don Miguel's estate. We had spent a lot of time together. "Father, the nagual also killed many cows at my master's estate last night."

"And you're going to tell me you saw it too!" the Father growled, angry at what he was hearing.

"No, but maybe Román did, but he didn't want to tell us anything. When I arrived to work this morning, all my colleagues were in the corral looking at those poor animals, and I also saw those tracks left by the nagual. Moreover, when we were coming back, we found many tracks identical to the ones we saw at the estate."

"Yes, it's true, Father," another confirmed as men and women began shouting and getting agitated.

"Besides, Father, how can you explain that every time something like this happens in other towns, many people start to disappear? Entire families, even children, and it only happens when the howls are heard. For years, nothing happens until they start to be heard again."

"They're just rumors," the cleric replied. "To make you feel more at ease, we'll hold special masses, and I'll go out to bless the streets. For now, return to work."

"No, Father!" they said. "We won't go back; the nagual has already marked them."

"Alright, as you wish, but stop thinking about it and let's say a prayer to ask God our Lord to protect us so that you feel more at ease."

I decided it was enough and asked to be taken to my estate.

At my estate, I waited for nightfall to return to Bocanegra's; I lay down to concentrate and see what was happening with the doctor at Don Miguel's house.

That place was completely silent, Sebastián saw no one. He knocked on the door, trembling from head to toe due to the silence of the place. He shouted, asking if anyone was there, but not even the dogs came out to bark as they usually did when someone arrived. He turned to leave when Román opened the door. The foreman was extremely gaunt, the dark circles under his eyes showed he hadn't slept. The doctor asked what was happening.

"Come in, Don Sebastián. My master is in his bedroom."

"Answer my question, Román."

"It's better if my master tells you himself."

They went upstairs; the doctor noticed blood stains on the wall. Román avoided looking at them, showing his fear as they passed. The doctor deduced that perhaps Don Miguel was injured. Behind the bedroom door, Don Miguel was sitting on the bed with his head down, Doña Lucía was crying, kneeling on the floor in front of her husband. Unsure how to ask, Bocanegra approached his host, while Doña Lucía quickly stood up and moved aside to let them be close. Don Miguel was sobbing.

"This can't be happening, why did it have to come now?"

I was sure he was referring to me, but I would find out too late whom he actually meant.

"What's going on?" Don Miguel lifted his head to look him in the eyes.

"Don't you know?"

"No," replied the doctor.

Don Miguel told him about his cattle pens, and that Román, upon seeing the beast, had shot at it without being able to injure it.

"Why didn't it attack you, Román?" questioned the visitor.

"I don't know," he responded, looking at the ground.

Don Miguel asked Doña Lucía to go check on their son and stay with him. Don Miguel didn't want his wife to hear what he was going to tell the doctor. As she left the room, Bocanegra still hadn't decided to tell him that the same thing had happened at his estate, wanting first to know what Don Miguel thought. The master asked Román to close the bedroom door from the inside, so their conversation wouldn't be heard.

"Do you remember a few months ago, at my birthday party, one of my workers came asking for your help?"

"Yes."

"He is the nagual; he came back for revenge." Don Miguel's

voice trembled.

"Please, there's no such thing as a nagual, they're just stories." But he also felt fear, though he denied accepting it could be true. "If it were true, why didn't he harm Román? He whipped him. Why are you so sure that dark-skinned man is now a nagual?"

"I don't know, maybe because Román was just following my orders, and he's after me. That night the wretch entered the room that's now my son's, after fighting with the foreman. It seems he leaned against the wall and left blood on it. The next day, I had it cleaned, but this morning it reappeared. Román painted the wall more than three times with water and lime to cover the blood, but it keeps resurfacing as if it were fresh all the time. Also, the water in the fountain turned red like that day, but it has since emptied, and I ordered not to refill it."

"Are you saying he came back to take revenge on us?"

"I already told you, maybe he's just after me."

"Two nights ago, at the end of the party I threw to welcome Don Josafat's nephew, something similar happened at my house. I think he just wants to scare us into leaving our lands."

"No, I don't believe that."

"Well, Don Miguel. I need you to allow Román to help me. My people also abandoned me, and I need to get rid of the dead animals. Another day, if my workers don't return, I'll try to get some from another town. I recommend you do the same."

"You can take him, just send him back before it gets dark. I don't want my family and I to be alone. Honestly, I don't know what I'm going to do. Tomorrow, I'll go talk to the priest to come and bless us."

"I'm deeply grateful; tomorrow I'll come to help you. We'll recover from this soon."

"As you say, doctor." Don Miguel was certain he couldn't escape from me and seemed to have lost his sanity. They said goodbye, and he didn't come out to see him off to the door as he always did with visitors.

On the way back, Román asked why he had thrown the party for Don Josafat's nephew.

"It's none of your business; no matter how much you want, you're still like those wretches, always so imprudent."

Despite the humiliation Román felt, he had to obey the orders to help the doctor at all costs. Sebastián Bocanegra believed that Josafat wanted to surprise his nephew, and they had paid him very well for the reception, understanding that Josafat didn't have the necessary servants at that time to attend to it. They continued in silence until they arrived.

By evening, Román and Bocanegra had finished placing the bodies as close together as they could, surrounding them with firewood. The doctor ordered Román to return to his master's house. Román felt more at ease, afraid of having to return alone in the dark. The landowner didn't even thank him for his help, feeling the favor was owed to Don Miguel.

Román mounted his horse and galloped away, not wanting to be caught by nightfall, fearing another encounter with the nagual.

Alone, the doctor carried dry hay bales and threw them over the animals, preparing to set them on fire. The smell of rotting flesh attracted many coyotes, who paced back and forth, trying to get closer. The man, enraged, picked up stones and threw them to scare them away.

"Get out of here!" he chased and cursed them, convinced they were responsible for the massacre. The dogs, having caught their scent, barked and chased them; the coyotes grew more numerous. Desperate, the doctor forgot to set the cattle remains on fire and ran to get a rifle.

"You'll pay for this!"

Transformed into an owl, I perched on a tree branch, watching. The dogs and coyotes, sensing my presence, howled. Inside the house, his wife protested.

"Don't go out, stay with me, I'm so scared because of those howls. You can finish tomorrow. It'll be safer in the daylight."

"Don't even think about it, they're just coyotes, and they'll pay right now."

The doctor checked the rifle to ensure it was loaded, stuffed more lead balls into his pocket, grabbed one of the lamps lighting the interior, and prepared to leave.

"Open the door, woman."

"For God's sake, listen to me, don't go out."

"I said open it."

When his wife finally opened the door, the dogs ran inside, making the woman scream.

"Cowardly brutes, I can take care of those coyotes myself!" he shouted furiously. "If you're so scared, lock yourself in the bedroom until I get back, you'll see how quickly I finish."

Walking briskly to where the cows were to be burned, the doctor heard the coyotes devouring them, the tearing of flesh making the stench even stronger and more unbearable.

From a distance, the doctor threw the lit lamp, and soon flames spread over the dead animals. The coyotes fled from the fire, stopping nearby; they stared at the doctor, the flames making their eyes glow, the only thing Bocanegra could distinguish of them. With my power, I made the wind blow to fan the fire.

The burning embers created infernal whirlwinds, the air currents pushing the fire toward the house, igniting the horse and cattle corrals with living animals inside.

The doctor dropped his weapon and ran to try to extinguish the flames, which spread quickly. He opened the corrals he could to save the animals that were trapped and burning alive.

The pyre had reached the trees near the house; branches fell onto the dwelling and the yard, preventing him from getting close to rescue his wife. Through one of the windows, he saw the woman screaming desperately; paralyzed with fear, the flames reached her when the roof collapsed, weakened by the fire.

The doctor, unable to do anything, watched her burn alive. Exhausted, he dropped to his knees, crying as I had when I lost my wife and child.

I descended from the tree and took human form, walking up to him silently. When I placed my hand on his shoulder, he quickly stood up and looked at me, incredulous. Noticing my calm demeanor, he stepped back, letting me feel the fear freezing his blood.

"What are you doing here?" he asked with a broken voice. I responded by circling him.

"In moments like these, how much we wish God were with us! We don't accept the idea that he didn't want to help us, we blame him for leaving us alone when we need him, we believe that only he has to do something for us or others because that's his job. If someone asks us for help, we think it's not our business. How do you ask God for a little help when you don't give it to anyone? Unless they have money to pay, because you don't take chickens or eggs, remember?" He started to back away without turning his back on me.

"No, Antonio, it can't be you." Terror gripped him.

"Doctor, I was that man you refused to help at Don Miguel's house. I'll show you what I am now," I said maliciously.

I transformed into the creature they called nagual; he ran to find his rifle, which he had dropped when the flames started spreading through the house. His favorite horse struggled to break free and escape the heat. The doctor ran, picked up his weapon, freed the steed, and with a leap, galloped as fast as he could in the opposite direction from where I was.

On my four legs, I marched to catch up to him. With one blow, I broke the horse's hindquarters, which, due to the speed, fell into the fire, throwing Sebastián Bocanegra onto the ground. I approached so he could see me.

"Forgive me, my God," he prayed, cried, and closed his eyes, trying not to see what was in front of him. The smell of his emotions excited me; feeling the panic he felt made me revel in his fear. I wanted to make his heart burst from fright. Just as he was about to lose consciousness, I pounced on him. He looked at me in horror as I devoured pieces of his flesh, trying to keep him alive as long as possible.

The horse didn't stop neighing and writhing in the flames consuming it as Sebastián Bocanegra died along with everything he loved.

My howls of satisfaction could be heard all the way to the town, while the villagers, seeing the glow of the fire, crossed themselves, imagining it all.

While I had my breakfast, after having taken the first step in my chain of revenge, I felt rested, even though my hatred for Don Miguel and Román was growing. I was scheming how to make them feel double the suffering they had caused me.

I savored the food as if it were the doctor's flesh, tasting his blood in my mouth as the most exquisite dish I had ever tasted. I wanted to taste human flesh again. I thought it had to be something tender, innocent, without a soul filled with the rot that feeds the debased. Like a true delicacy, someone I didn't know but knew existed came to my mind, someone who was part of the alliance I made with Josafat.

Don Miguel would go to town to speak with the priest. Why chase what I wanted to catch when I could wait for it where it would arrive?

I called for my carriage. I thought of spending the whole day with the clergyman so that Don Miguel wouldn't have the opportunity to speak until late in the afternoon. Through the priest, I would know what was discussed and what would happen at the Hacienda, if I could convince the priest to go bless them.

In town, the pilgrimage to glorify the streets had already ended, and although people knew about the fire, none dared accompany the ecclesiastic to find out the condition of the Bocanegras.

I got down and approached the man to introduce myself and ensnare him. He was still talking to one of the locals, who was asking him not to go near the hacienda because they were likely dead, that he wouldn't even find a trace, that the evil might be there, and anyone could be its victim, even him.

"Look, son, divine strength is with us, it protects us from all evil, and it's our duty to look out for others' well-being. We must find out if the doctor and his wife need help, but since neither you nor anyone else wants to accompany me, I'll go alone."

"I only hope your faith protects you from what has started to darken these places," and he bid farewell.

"Go with God, my son, and stop talking nonsense about that nagual."

I approached the Father, extending my hand.

"Good morning, Father. I am Antonio Vizcarra, Josafat's nephew. I arrived recently and wanted to come meet you, my uncle spoke much about you before leaving for Spain. He recommended that while he was gone, I should turn to you, that I wouldn't find a better person for advice." He looked at me as if I were familiar to him.

"Son, maybe it's the resemblance to your uncle, it feels like I've known you for a long time. But anyway, welcome and though it's not the best time to say it, you can come see me whenever you need."

"Why, Father? What worries you? Is there something I could do for you?"

"Look, son, people are very scared about some things. But the worst happened last night, I found out after the pilgrimage about what happened at the Bocanegra Hacienda, and from what I see, you don't know anything either."

"No, Father, what happened?" I feigned surprise.

"All I know is there was a fire last night, and I don't really know if it was at the doctor's hacienda. I want to make sure, but no one will accompany me, and at my age, it's too much to go alone."

"Please, Father, allow me to offer my help. We can go in my car. Although I've known the doctor for a short time, I'd like to know if they need anything."

"Thank God there are good people like you, son, who care about their fellow man, God will reward you."

"Father, let's not waste any more time and go see the doctor and his wife," I said to hurry him.

On the way, I told the priest my version of the life I had led in Spain and the reason that made me decide to live with my uncle Josafat.

The place was desolate, the air carried death. Only the walls of the majestic building remained standing, its ashes carried by the light wind, erasing what had really happened. The priest crossed himself as he got out of the car.

"For the heart of Jesus, what happened here?"

He walked among the still hot and smoking debris, looking for signs of the couple. In what had been the stable and where the fire had started, the scene was grotesque, the sight of what hadn't been consumed was terrifying, as if the place were part of hell, and the charred bodies belonged to souls condemned to burn in it. The priest covered his mouth and nose with his hand, avoiding breathing the nauseating smell while I, without letting my satisfaction show, savored the scent of revenge.

He began to pray for the souls of the doctor and his wife, something I would not allow. I stepped back, staying behind the priest, and quietly recited my spells.

The wind lifted the ashes, getting into the priest's mouth and nose, preventing him from continuing his prayers. The sky filled with black clouds, threatening to unleash a storm.

"We better leave, because if it starts to rain, we won't be able to get out, it will be very difficult for the horses to pull. We better come back tomorrow."

In the vehicle, the priest could breathe better.

"May God keep them in his holy glory," he said, convinced they hadn't survived. "I'll pray for their souls' rest and ask for the forgiveness of their sins. Tomorrow I'll hold a special mass for them." To buy more time, I invited him to lunch at my estate, claiming I had some pending matters, and if I took him first, I wouldn't have enough time to finish them. "Son, if you want, we can go to your house first, but I can't accept lunch. With what we've seen, I feel a stomachache, if I eat something, it won't sit well. Better tell your driver to take me as soon as we get to your house, I'll accept the invitation another day."

"As you wish, Father, but I hope you'll join me very soon," I replied, pleased with his kind and concerned response. Upon arrival, I said goodbye to the priest, the storm clouds had already cleared from the sky.

I transformed into a raven and flew to Don Miguel's Hacienda. I perched on the rooftop, waiting to see if he would meet with the priest. The dogs, as always, barked and howled in fear at my presence until they ran away, making the place even more silent. After almost an hour of waiting, I finally saw:

"Father, I've been waiting for you almost all day. I didn't want to leave without speaking to you." "Tell me, son, why do you need me?" "Father, for the love of God, I need you to come to my house. I'll explain the urgency on the way." Don Miguel nearly dragged the priest into the carriage. "Wait, son, you don't know what happened at the doctor's Hacienda." Tired from the day's exertions, the priest hoped Don Miguel would desist from taking him away. Don Miguel's skin prickled— "Last night there was a fire on his land, and I just returned from there, trying to find out what happened. But what I found gives me no hope that he or his wife are alive." "Father, that's why I want you to come to my house." Noticing his desperation, the priest decided to accompany him.

"Alright, son, let's go. Tell me what's going on." "Thank you, Father," he sighed in relief. "Please, bring your things to bless my house." The priest reminded him it wasn't necessary as the hacienda had already been blessed. Don Miguel insisted he do it again. "Alright, son, let me get inside, and then we'll leave."

Don Miguel's anxiety grew as the night began to cover them. As soon as the priest returned, Don Miguel ordered Román to hasten the horses. Don Miguel recounted the massacre of the animals and his last conversation with the doctor. He said he suspected who the nagual was, and the priest asked his reasons. Don Miguel didn't tell the truth, only that the doctor had refused to help the laborer and that he had merely fired him.

"Just because you fired him, you think that man could be a Nagual? Look, son, you must not be influenced by the natives. These are myths people invent, burdened by fear and guilt from their sins."

Sensing their approach, I entered the house through one of the windows, flying to the bedroom where Don Miguel's son slept. Doña Lucía was finishing preparing dinner for her husband. In raven form, I perched over the baby's crib and began to transform into a cruel entity. The weight of my body shattered the crib, and under my claws, the baby fell, crying out from the impact.

Hearing the noise, Doña Lucía dropped what she was holding and ran towards us. As she climbed the stairs, she slipped and broke her leg while rolling down. She climbed back up, dragging herself step by step. Her son began to be torn apart by my jaws. The baby's blood pooled, leaving my footprints marked on the floor. When she reached the door, she saw me devouring her son's flesh. Her eyes bulged, and she screamed, driven mad by terror.

Don Miguel, the priest, and Román, hearing the woman's screams, rushed inside as I exited through one of the windows, breaking it as I leaped out. The wind through the broken window extinguished the candles lighting the room. When they reached Doña Lucía, I was on the rooftop waiting for their reaction.

The mother thrashed on the floor, trying to fend off the men who were trying to help her; she felt they were my claws, the same ones that had torn her son apart. Román entered the child's room, but in the dim light, he didn't see the blood on the floor and slipped, falling next to one of the baby's limbs. Realizing what had happened, he quickly stood up to prevent Don Miguel from entering, hugging him tightly to stop his advance, but the master pushed Román aside and continued inside. Don Miguel began to shout in despair. The priest left Doña Lucía and ran to where the Spaniard was.

The priest covered his mouth to contain the panic that escaped from deep within his soul, crossed himself, and began to pray. Throwing holy water, the windows shattered into pieces. The priest, Román, and Don Miguel were expelled by an evil force from the room where the baby's remains were. The gusts of wind blowing through the broken windows extinguished all the candles and lamps illuminating the house, toppling everything in their path, until reaching Don Miguel's wife. The dark sky began to be lit by lightning strikes, briefly illuminating the inside of the house. Doña Lucía was being dragged by an invisible force along the walls and ceiling, lifted and slammed to the floor repeatedly, while the priest sprinkled holy water over her, trying to free her from that threat. The furniture shook as if in an earthquake, Don Miguel and Román clung to the priest's legs, feeling they were also being dragged. I jumped from the rooftop to the main door, in their sight.

A lightning flash illuminated my figure at the fountain; in the darkness, they could only see the glint of my eyes disappearing as I moved away to avoid being seen further. The priest continued to pray until everything fell silent. Doña Lucía lay unconscious on the floor. The three of them returned to Don Miguel's son's room, but when they relit the candles to illuminate the place, they discovered the remains had disappeared. The only things left were the bloodstains and my footprints marked on the floor.

They turned to where they had left Doña Lucía, who had also disappeared. They couldn't explain how she wasn't there anymore. It was impossible she had gotten up on her own without making any noise. They searched anxiously throughout the house, calling her name, but nothing responded.

Román took a lamp to go outside; the priest and Don Miguel said they would accompany him, that it was better to stay together until dawn. In the courtyard, they saw the woman's figure, tied to the fountain in the same way I had been, kneeling with her head resting on the fountain.

Doña Lucía's dress was torn, her bare back covered in wounds, as if she had been whipped like I had been. Her long hair covered her neck, hiding the worst damage, which Don Miguel discovered as he knelt beside her, hugging her body to comfort her.

The woman's head rolled to Román's feet. The horror Román felt seeing Doña Lucía's open eyes accusing him of what had been done to me; he dropped the lamp while Don Miguel cried out in the same desperation I had on that fateful night. But his despair was greater, knowing it was my vengeance.

The strong wind quickly spread the fire, reaching Don Miguel and Doña Lucía's remains. Román and the priest tried to put out the flames while dragging him to safety. I decided to leave the place.

Don Miguel's burns were severe, but he would survive; Doña Lucía's remains turned to ashes, extinguishing with the arrival of the new sun. Don Miguel, Román, and the priest stayed outside the house all night, while I enjoyed everything I saw from my perch. The priest, after blessing the house while Román watched over Don Miguel outside, instructed the foreman to take his master to rest, to check his injuries.

The priest tended to Don Miguel in his bedroom.

"Son, I agree that what we experienced tonight is something infernal, the evil one has been here, but please, I want you to tell me the truth about what happened with the one you say is a nagual. What did you do to him? I want you to tell me. You've already lost your family, and I want to know under the oath of confession, and if I ask you this way, it's because I only want to help you. I don't blame you for your family's death, nor for what you have done, because everything is by God's hand; He does not make mistakes nor allows things to happen without His consent. What makes you think he is responsible for what happened last night?" In the eyes of the religious man, Don Miguel had always been a very charitable and good person. I thought that, for the first time, he would show the priest the kind of person he truly was. I thought I would hear words of repentance, at least in memory of his loved ones, that he would feel remorse for what they had done to me. But what he began to recount made my blood boil; not even the loss of his family had cleansed the rot from his soul. At all costs, he wanted to maintain his image of an unblemished man. With tears in his eyes, he answered.

"You know how I am, the night the laborer arrived, my wife had organized a party to celebrate my birthday; I don't know how he got into my house, but he asked the doctor, rest his soul, to help him because his wife was about to give birth. I don't know why he didn't ask me; I would have gladly helped him, that boy was very dear to me, I saw him grow up. When the doctor refused to assist him, he went mad and started insulting my guests; with all the pain in my heart, I had to throw him out; I planned to receive him the next day, but he never returned. Truly, Father, if you say that everything that happens is by the hand of God, I don't understand why He allows good people like us to go through things like this, for innocent ones like my son to die in such an unjust and cruel way. My wife and I were not to blame for the doctor's refusal to help him."

"Look, our children, from the moment they are born, carry the faults we have committed," replied the priest, not entirely believing him. "That's why before they are born, it's necessary for the father and mother to confess and sincerely ask for forgiveness for their sins, so they do not inherit them. Baptism only frees them from the sin with which they were conceived, but the sins we continue to commit in life will accumulate in our descendants. As for your wife, I'll explain it this way: if we as sinners do not confess our sins and do not repent, any loved one of ours can unwittingly become a martyr, to pay for us and make us suffer for their loss. But for direct sinners, the punishment we receive will be even harsher, for we will be condemned to burn in hell for all eternity, so I hope you are telling me the truth."

"That is the truth, Father, what I've told you is how things happened." He seemed to believe his own lie. The priest was disappointed.

"Well, son, I must leave, I will ask Román to take me to the village, I feel exhausted. I will return another day to see how you are doing, and if you need me before then, send for me and I will come right away. Before I leave, tell me what you plan to do from now on."

"As soon as I can get up, I will try to sell, I don't want to stay here. I have a pending matter, but Román will handle it. Thank you, Father, for what you have done."

The priest left the hacienda, and I was content to hear that Don Miguel would stay there for a while longer. It would take him quite some time to recover and find a buyer. Román had to dispose of the cows, the rotting meat had attracted thousands of flies, and the hacienda had a decadent appearance in every corner.

That pending matter left me thoughtful. I never imagined it would become the most important thing in my life, and without giving it much importance, I decided to take some time to rest. I knew they would not live in peace, the priest would visit them sooner or later, and I would find out if there was anything that interested me to continue my vengeance.

After a couple of days at my hacienda, I decided to spend some time in a town about ten hours away. I wanted to go to that place because I didn't know it and they would be having their patronal festivities.

I wouldn't have any trouble settling in; Josafat had acquired properties there, as in many other places. With the power he gave me, I also received his material assets, which I had to pass on to the one who would take my place. With the money from the profits, I had to buy more houses so that the next person could move wherever they pleased.

I wished to finish my revenge soon, and I thought that maybe in that place I could find my successor. As I crossed its streets to reach the house where I would stay, people stared in admiration and envy at my carriage. Its black color shone, highlighted by the gold frames and moldings, the pure silver candlesticks on the sides reflecting the sun's rays, dazzling, and the crest on the doors engraved in the wood. It was the head of a coyote with an open skull, in whose center was embedded a perfectly polished quartz stone, symbol of the first who obtained the power to defeat his enemies.

My coachman pulled the carriage in front of the house, located right in the center of the town. The heavy wooden door opened, and the servants who would attend to me were waiting; they recognized their new master just by seeing who got out of the vehicle. They immediately put themselves at my service, but all I wanted was to rest from the long journey, and I headed to my bedroom.

When I lay down, memories came flooding in. My losses turned to nothing but resentment; the price of my power began to seem very high to me. Regret ran through my mind without knowing what to do. Despite my strength and wealth, I felt empty, unable to find meaning in continuing; ending the lives of those who had hurt me made me feel miserable, but I also knew I had to fulfill the deal I had accepted. I let a few days pass, thinking I would soon make a decision.

In the past few days, I hadn't learned anything new about Don Miguel and Román. The village priest hadn't gone to see them, and I had no desire to go on my own.

When the festivities began, I went out for a walk. My thoughts flew, imagining that the woman I had loved and the child I never knew were by my side, enjoying the same landscape I saw. I imagined my wife holding my arm while our son ran around causing mischief, trying to explore the world around him as we laughed at what he did when he found something and turned to look at us surprised, as if saying, "I didn't know this," and after understanding what he had in his hands, he would run to embrace us both, wishing we were together forever.

But love arrived once more when before my eyes appeared that sweet woman, with an angelic face and divine smile, honest and sincere, the smile of someone who, by just giving it, compensates for any bad weather, just to enjoy the moment of her presence. That was the angel who appeared in the midst of the hell that was my life. Nervousness overwhelmed me, surpassing my confidence. I felt insignificant seeing her beauty; I didn't know how to approach her without offending her with my audacity to address her. The gift of her smile disarmed me, possible words disappeared, leaving me with the impression of her good feelings. I was confused to the point of losing my sense of reality, the fear of taking a wrong step silenced me, leaving me with the hope of a clearer sign indicating the precise moment to declare the feelings that had awakened.

Fireworks shot up from the ground to explode, illuminating the shadows with different colors, like granted wishes. Just like one of mine.

The woman who had captivated me stopped in the middle of the street to give a sugar candy to a barefoot child watching the lights in the sky. In the background, a man started screaming as a firework exploded in his hand, shattering it; his horse, frightened by the noise, broke free from the reins and ran uncontrollably down the street, heading straight for the lady and the child. Without thinking, I reacted by throwing myself toward them to get them out of the path of the runaway horse. I turned my body so they would fall on me and cushion the impact.

As we fell, I longed for a new life. The darkness of my past vanished when those beautiful eyes illuminated mine and made me lose myself in the abyss of love, believing that the woman in my arms would share the rest of her life with me. For several seconds, we looked directly at each other, I enjoyed the scent of her breath, wishing the distance between her lips and mine would disappear. Those around us watched, moved, feeling the tenderness that was beginning to awaken in our hearts.

The child's cry in our arms woke us up; we stood up slowly without taking our eyes off each other. I held her as if she were a delicate flower petal. The little one ran to his mother's arms.

"Are you alright?" we asked at the same time and smiled shyly when we realized the coincidence and that we were still holding hands. We walked together, looking at nothing. I asked her name, the tone of her voice sounded like a caress to my wounded soul. Ángela, perfect for that cherub who was putting together the pieces of the heart that cruel fate had shattered.

I didn't know what name to introduce myself with, whether to tell her my name or the one Josafat had given me. I didn't want to tarnish the purity of that moment with a lie, knowing I couldn't tell her who I was, and if I lied, I would have to do so for as long as I was with her. The fear of losing her company made me deceitful.

Crossing the square, for us, there were no people or the noise of the celebration. I wanted to know everything about her, and I asked if we could sit on one of the benches.

Not knowing where to start the conversation, I asked about her family and if she lived in the town. Sadness was drawn on her face when she said her mother had died when she was born. I regretted the question upon sensing the nostalgia she felt talking about her mother, it broke my heart. The last thing I wanted was to cause her the slightest sorrow, she was like a beautiful crystal figure, and I didn't want her to break. I apologized immediately.

"Don't worry, that happened a long time ago, I just try to live loving her the way I would if she were with me. I only have my father, whom I haven't seen in years when he used to visit me; I've lived my whole life in Spain. The only family I've had with me are my uncles and three cousins. I just arrived from Spain to meet my father, but he doesn't live here, and while we reunite, I'm staying at a friend's house, and for now, I don't know how long I'll be in the town."

The fact that I had very little time to convince her to stay by my side forever produced a terrible anguish in me, I didn't know how to propose that she allow me to see her, nor how she might take my words. My anxiety disappeared when she asked me to accompany her to where she was staying. With great effort, I hid the joy I felt hearing her, but I invited her to lunch the next day; her excitement in accepting indicated to me that she had the same feeling that had taken hold of me.

She asked me to leave her at a certain distance, not wanting her father's friends to ask questions upon seeing her arrive with someone, preferring we wait so she could introduce me properly. We set the time and place where we would meet at noon and parted, making the promise that we would be punctual. The idea of a better future flooded me, growing like the love for the woman I had just met. In my bedroom, the temptation to use my energy to know what she was doing tempted me. I decided not to use anything unnatural because I didn't want the evil within me to touch her. I didn't know if the love for my late wife had ended or if I was simply very sensitive from losing her. Maybe the desire to love and be loved had occupied me all my life due to my lonely childhood, and I let myself be carried away.

From the moment I woke up, I eagerly awaited the hour of my date. I got up to organize everything necessary; I wanted us to have lunch in the countryside.

I requested my carriage to be prepared, took the basket with everything I would share with the woman who had captivated me, and set out to meet her. The day was the brightest and most beautiful, but it couldn't compare to the perfection of finding her.

She awaited me with a basket in hand, and I couldn't help but think that our thoughts had harmonized. I greeted Ángela with a kiss on the hand and opened the carriage door, inviting her to get in and indicating that we should be taken to the outskirts. We talked about how we had met, arguing that the stars had brought us together. She had never imagined coming from Spain to live with her father, but suddenly the need grew until she decided to do so. I admitted that it was my first time there; I told her I had grown up in one of my uncle's houses because I lost my parents in an accident when I was only seven years old, and the only person I had been with was my uncle Josafat. I denied the story the teacher had told, saying I had come to that place because my uncle's hacienda was in a very isolated spot and he was traveling, trying to distract me and enjoy the region's festivities. We found the perfect spot for us.

"How beautiful it is here!" We got out to contemplate the landscape, and she decided we should stay. The driver took the horses to graze while we had lunch and decided when to return to the town.

Many more perfect days like that passed until we gave ourselves to each other, believing we would be together forever. I had forgotten my revenge and the resentment towards Don Miguel and Román; I only thought day by day about the love I was living. I insisted on meeting the people she lived with, wanting to meet her father. I was willing to do anything to get her family's permission to see her without hiding and to marry her. I was afraid of losing her. One day she sent me a letter.

"Antonio:

I have fallen madly in love, but our love has no future. My father sent word that I will soon be reunited with him, and that I must be prepared because he will send for me. He is sick and I cannot leave him alone; I must obey his orders. Please, do not seek me out anymore. Knowing that I will never be able to be with you again takes away my will to live; I find no meaning in my life without you. But I also cannot abandon my father. I will return to Spain with him. Forgive me for not being able to say these words to you in person, but I hope you understand that the pain I am causing you, I am suffering even more because I will never love anyone as I love you. Your memory will always be with me, and I will love you forever and above all; my heart stays with you.

Eternally, Ángela."

When I finished reading, I collapsed. I didn't understand how, if Ángela loved me, we couldn't be together. I was sure that the money I had could make her father accept our marriage. But the decision was not her father's, but hers, and in all the time we were together, Ángela didn't care about what I had; she only fell in love with me. I realized that whatever I could say to her wouldn't change her mind.

I had written a poem to give her when we met, thinking it was my heart where I wrote it, before reading Ángela's letter. My tears blurred the ink drawn on the paper, and I clenched it in my hand with all my strength, trying to squeeze out the feeling I had put into it, and threw it to the ground.

I spent the night crying, sitting next to the table where I read the letter. The door to my room opened. I didn't lift my gaze. I remained head down, sobbing, not wanting to know what the person who had entered wanted.

Ángela had picked up the piece of paper I had thrown, and she came closer, reading.

"You are the light of my life, you fill me with love every day, you are the divine force that has erased the darkness in which I lived,

and if I lose you, my life, mine would end."

Tears streamed down her cheeks as she ran to embrace me. I held her tightly to my body, not wanting to believe that what her letter said was true. I wanted to hear that it had all been a joke or that we would find a solution. However, she dried my tears with her fingers while I moved my head to keep my face in her hands, and her words pierced me like a sword.

"I don't want you to suffer; it also hurts me to know that we have to part, but I want you to try to be strong. The time by your side has been the most beautiful I have lived, you are the only man I have loved. The love I feel for you is even stronger than the affection I have for my father, but understand that I have to stay with him, and he wants to return to Spain. I can't tell you to come with us; the disappointment of knowing what I have done would kill him. He wouldn't understand my reasons for asking him to let you come with us. I wanted to see you one last time to ask for your forgiveness and to let you know that I am also suffering from this separation, and that the memory of what I lived with you will always live by my side." She slowly moved away from me. How was it possible that Ángela had the strength and courage to leave me if she loved me as much as I loved her? I thought she had never loved me and only felt guilty for the pain she was causing me. I watched her leave without asking her to stay with me. The decision was hers, and I had a deal to fulfill. Perhaps with her in my life, I wouldn't be able to complete it. I hoped time would heal my wounds, but every attempt to forget her was in vain. I returned to the estate I had obtained from Josafat, driven to feed my soul with the hatred I felt for Román and Don Miguel.

A few days later, the image of the priest with Román, the church in my town, came to my mind.

"Father, I've come to tell you that Don Miguel has made a deal to sell the estate. At dawn tomorrow, we will leave; I'm going with him, and I don't plan to ever return. My master sends his thanks for everything you did for him, and he asked me to say goodbye on his behalf. I must go now, we have to finish preparing the last things for our journey."

"Son, say goodbye to Don Miguel for me. I wish you both luck and may God bless you and go with you wherever you go."

I realized I had forgotten everything. I had to kill Don Miguel to force Román to stay, and then I would only have to follow Román's steps until I found someone to take my place.

I waited for darkness to fall so I could go and watch them. They wouldn't dare leave their house at night; they would depart at sunrise.

I arrived transformed into a wolf at the outskirts where the main road was, from there I could follow them in any direction they took. While I waited for the right moment to attack, the memories of the past few months tormented me desperately, even for the loss of Ángela, I held them responsible.

Finally, I distinguished Don Miguel's wagon. Román held

the rifle in his hand, urging the horses to move faster away from the place they considered cursed. I followed them from a distance so the horses wouldn't notice me. As I traveled the road, the trees reminded me of the night I lost my wife and son. By my spells, the rain began to fall, black clouds covered the sky, preventing the sun from illuminating the morning; lightning struck the ground near the wagon until one of them split a tree in half, which fell on top of them. The impact broke the axle, overturning the wagon with the wheels to the side. Román rolled a few meters away. Without stopping my advance, I transformed into the leviathan they wanted to avoid.

Román was getting up while Don Miguel crawled out of the free door, searching for balance in a crouch. I swiftly leapt onto his back, throwing him onto the ground near his foreman. Román shot at me, making me furious. With one swipe, I tore off his arm along with the rifle, leaving him collapsed on his knees, trying to stop the bleeding with his remaining hand. Before their eyes, I regained my human form. Recognizing me and despite the fear, Don Miguel accused me of killing his wife and son. I reminded them of what they made me endure, what I found upon arriving at my house after being whipped at the fountain, and that under the pact I made, I couldn't leave any heirs of my tormentors alive, now victims, because I had been forced to accept this power with the loss of my son, my first descendant.

"Wait for me in hell..." I lunged. A familiar voice shouted to stop me. Ángela, who had seen and heard everything.

"If you kill him, you'll have to kill me too, he is my father."

Feeling her and reading her mind, I knew something had changed. Her life depended on my decision, and I couldn't bring myself to kill the woman I loved. Nor the child of mine she carried within her. After discovering what she had growing inside, I wanted to approach her, but the fear I caused her was terrible. To her eyes, I was no longer the man she loved but the beast. The desperation was making me lose control, I couldn't bear the thought that in the end, the life of the woman I loved and my unborn child would have to die by my claws. It was the same feeling of loss that started all this evil.

I fled to where I had buried my family, over their grave, begging for forgiveness for what I had done. The rain answered my laments.

At dusk, I locked myself in my room trying to erase the past, but the clairvoyant visions made me face reality.

Román had bled to death at the scene, they were helped by a family also traveling. They were told that the tree had killed Román and caused Don Miguel's injuries, that she hadn't noticed the accident because she was asleep and was knocked out by the crash.

They carried Román's body covered with a blanket. They continued assisted until the next town, where the doctor confirmed to Ángela that her father wouldn't survive. In his agony, Don Miguel made his daughter swear she would return to Spain and never come back. She didn't tell him she had met me.

In her last months of pregnancy, she secluded herself in a convent to bring my child into the world. For many nights, I watched her caressing her belly, hoping that the father's evil wouldn't touch her child. Ángela continued to remember and love me until she died on the day of childbirth. The last thing I saw of her was when she gave a final kiss to our son, whose face gradually faded from my mind.

98

—That's my story, Father, the only person who can kill me is someone of my own blood, who joined with that of the man for whom I accepted the pact with Jehoshaphat. I had tried to forget, life was going on as normally as a tormented man can have, that all I had to do was wait for me to meet one of my kind who would finish me off.

Years later, while I was walking down the street, I saw a man and his face stuck in my mind. At night, while he slept, images of the atrocities he had caused to another made me feel the sorrow of the one who had just died in my dreams. I woke up thinking it had been a nightmare, but the pain I felt was real. I used my power to find out more. The guy I saw was a murderer.

I spent many days enduring the discomfort in my soul, I refused to kill the evil one that I had visualized, but one night, without having control, I transformed into the beast, as if someone or something forced me to do what I did not want. Conscious at all times I went for him, determined. By killing him, I regained control and understood that while I found my killer, I had to take the place of those who could have accepted mine.

Therefore, Father, as I find the end of my existence, every time someone sells their soul to the devil to get revenge on another, I am the one who has to do the work. Over time, I have learned to absorb the pain of good people who, by accepting the obligation, transmit it to me, and when I have to eliminate the targets, I enjoy it.

I have had to live in different places trying to find my blood successor to free myself from this curse in which I trapped myself. In each place I plant memories in the minds of the people around me that make them think they know me. I have infiltrated many families, making them believe that I belong to them. Then I disappear and erase the memories. I stop my search when I have to end the life of someone who harmed another who before dying was free of sin. I became the avenging angel that I played at being when I was a child, and although I work for the opposite side, it gives me the satisfaction of saying that I can wait as long as necessary, until I find the end of my destiny. With each passing day, the idea that I was a normal man disappears. I have come to think that I have always been the one who was my teacher, and that the story of how he found me and transformed me is something that I have invented to maintain the hope that I will be able to end this way of living and free me

—So, my son, if what you just told me is true, I can sell my soul to your master and obtain the power you say you have. Have you told others?

—Yes, Father, I have told others, when it is their turn to pay for their sins, and you cannot make a deal to get what I have.

-What are you saying?

—Don't you understand, Father? Why make a deal with a soul that is already condemned to burn in hell? I come for you. — The priest stood up shouting as he left the confessional.

—No, what you're telling me can't be true, you're crazy, help! Help!-

"Scream, Father, scream," I said, as I began my physical transformation, "who do you think created the rain that is falling outside?" Why do you think there is no one else in this church? For many years you abused many children, until one of your victims committed suicide because she could no longer bear his attacks. The girl was ten years old and she left a letter; In her innocent words she did not realize that the one she blamed was her own father. The police arrested him, accused of paying for the death of his daughter. Do you have any idea what they both suffered? I do. And what awaits you is much worse than you can imagine. Keep running, Father, you have no salvation anyway.

—No, demon, you cannot enter the House of God.

—The House of God is within us, Father, and both you and I close it with our actions. Listen to the police sirens, Father. They are coming for you. They have already reported you, but they will not find you alive. He will run towards the altar, I will fall on him and break him into pieces in front of the cross of Christ.

-No no no...!!